Greater Than a Tourist – Cumbria and The Lake District, United Kingdom

50 Travel Tips from a Local

Kerry Thornton

Lock Haven, PA
All rights reserved.
ISBN: 9781522063353

>TOURIST

Kerry Thornton

BOOK DESCRIPTION

Are you excited about planning your next trip? Do you want to try something new while traveling? Would you like some guidance from a local? If you answered yes to any of these questions, then this book is just for you.

Cumbria and the Lake District by Kerry Thornton offers the inside scope on this beautiful region in England. Most travel books tell you how to travel like a tourist. Although there's nothing wrong with that, as a part of the Greater than a Tourist series, this book will give you travel tips from someone who lives at your next travel destination.

In these pages you'll discover local advice that will help you throughout your stay. This book will not tell you exact addresses or store hours but instead will give you an excitement and knowledge from a local that you may not find in other smaller print travel books. Travel like a local. Slow down, stay in one place, and get to know the people and the culture of a place.

By the time you finish this book, you will be eager and prepared to travel to your next destination.

Kerry Thornton

TABLE OF CONTENTS

BOOK DESCRIPTION

TABLE OF CONTENTS

DEDICATION

FROM THE PUBLISHER

WELCOME TO > TOURIST

INTRODUCTION

1. Awards won by Cumbria and The Lakes District

2. The Regional Capital - Carlisle

3. The Scottish Border

4. The Lakes

5. Coniston

6. Wastwater

7. Thirlmere

8. Lake Cruises

9. Derwentwater

10. Windermere

11. The Beaches

12. The Forests

13. The Wildlife

14. Predator Experience

15. The Mountains

16. The Three Peaks Challenge

17. The Pennines

18. Camping or Glamping

19. The Railways

20. The Passes

21. The Arts and Artists of the Lakes

22. Beatrix Potter

23. Brockhole

24. Wordsworth

25. History

26. Bronze Age History

27. Roman History

28. Rheged

29. Castles

30. Monasteries, Abbeys and Cathedrals

31. Georgian and Victorian Homes

32. Museums

33. Art Galleries

34. Gardens and Parks

35. Farms

36. Spas

37. Family orientated activities

38. Leisure Centres

39. General Entertainment

40. Aquariums

41. Centre Parcs

42. Food and Drink

43. Kendal Mint Cake

44. The Rum Story

45. The Weather

46. Travelling with Disabilities

47. Travelling with Pets

48. Traditions of Cumbria

49. Language and Pronunciations

50. But wait…there's more…

Top Reasons to Book This Trip

WHERE WILL YOU TRAVEL TO NEXT?

Our Story

DEDICATION

This book is dedicated to my family who don't know where my travel bug and itchy feet came from but support it nevertheless.

Kerry Thornton

ABOUT THE AUTHOR

Kerry mainly grew up in Cumbria and her immediate family still reside there. When she visits the UK she sees them and this beautiful region. When she returns the weather is always sunny to fool her into thinking that all those childhood memories of the drizzly, cold rain for weeks on end were false. The towns are expanding and the demographics of the population are rapidly changing in this area but overall it's still very different from the rest of England. The protected area of the Lakes District National Park will hopefully prevent the regions beauty being swallowed up in the fires of industry.

Kerry loves to travel and has lived abroad in several countries. Kerry runs her own occupational therapy private practice. Kerry works with families who are struggling with the significant illness or injury in the family. She helps the whole family adjust and live well. If this sounds like something that will benefit you or someone you know you can find Kerry on LinkedIn www.linkedin.com/in/kerry-thornton-63335471/.

Kerry Thornton

HOW TO USE THIS BOOK

This book was written by someone who has lived in an area for over three months. The author has made the best suggestions based on their own experiences in the area. Please check that these places are still available before traveling to the area. The goal of this book is to help travelers either dream or experience different locations by providing opinions from a local.

Kerry Thornton

FROM THE PUBLISHER

Traveling can be one of the most important moments in a person's life. The memories that you have of anticipating going somewhere new or getting to travel are some of the best. As a publisher of the Greater Than a Tourist book series, as well as the popular 50 Things to Know book series, we strive to help you learn about new places, spark your imagination, and inspire you.

Thought this book you will find something for every traveler. Wherever you are and whatever you do I wish you safe fun, and inspiring travel.

Lisa Rusczyk Ed. D.
CZYK Publishing

Kerry Thornton

WELCOME TO > TOURIST

Kerry Thornton

INTRODUCTION

Cumbria and the Lake District are not the same place. Cumbria is the county, the Lake District a region within it, and the Lake District National Park is a further protected area within that county. Most visitors will not leave the Lake District region but the Cumbrian towns outside the boundaries do still have activities, charm, and even festivals.

Since I grew up there the amount of things to do in this region has increased 10 fold so any visitors are well catered for. You will see people who only hike the hills, only canoe the waterways, only visit the towns, only appreciate the history and all of them can be totally content with their time in this region. I've included a variety of ideas based upon my own experiences but still there is more available than 50 tips can cover. The place names and activities mentioned are easy to search on the internet to get the most updated information.

Kerry Thornton

1. Awards won by Cumbria and The Lakes District

I hope you read the introduction so you know the difference between Cumbria and the Lake District! If not skip back there so you can see where you will find award winning places.

As awards are only as good as the year they are won, and places may not exist despite great accolades, suffice to say that

- Cumbrian businesses have consistently won awards in VisitEngland Awards for Excellence.
- Business within Cumbria compete against each other for the Cumbria Tourism Awards.
- There are four Michellin Starred restaurants in the Lakes District.
- The scenery wins awards for beauty in popularity polls.

2. The Regional Capital - Carlisle

Carlisle is brimming with activities and it is all about history. It had Roman, Celtic, Viking and Tudor influences to name a few.

One of my favourite school trips was to Carlisle Castle because of a live action tour but perhaps they don't try as hard to be entertaining for adults – you'll have to let me know! The Military Museum there is a separate fee but holds the most information because the castle itself is mainly rooms and views. It's good to dress warmly because there's lots of outside areas / cold rooms and it's a few hundred metres walk from the car park / city streets.

Tullie House in a museum and Art gallery with a café. It is small but nicely presented and perfect if the weather is bad for a few hours.

Carlisle Cathedral has services and the occasional concerts. It's full of 15th Century art and beautiful stained glass windows.

The Sands Centre has the city's fitness facilities and a live entertainment venue for theatre, music, dance, comedy. The quality of the available entertainment has improved immeasurably since I was a child and my parents are now always up there seeing something or other.

Many locals from across Cumbria make the big trip to Carlisle for the day to go shopping. When we were growing up a trip to Carlisle was a special occasion. Now public transport and the roads have improved it's a bit less of a big deal.

3. The Scottish Border

Hadrian's wall was the border between England and Scotland for many years but now the political border is slightly higher. Still you can stand at the top of Hadrian's wall on a good day and see a long way – possibly to Scotland but most likely more of Northumberland!

It is a UNESCO world heritage site and to visit here is to marvel at what the Roman soldiers achieved without the modern technology we have nowadays. To get to the Visitors Centre you technically enter Northumberland so it depends how much you want to know and see of the wall.

There is no obvious border marking with Scotland (at the moment) so only a sign will tell you that you've made the transition.

4. The Lakes

There is one "Lake" in the Lake District – Bassenthwaite Lake! The rest contain mere, water or tarn in their names making 15 other main lakes but there's even more than that around! Using this knowledge to impress friends will not go unappreciated.

At basically every lake (except Ennerdale Water, Haweswater and Thirlmere) you can swim (in the cold water), walk along a beach and fish (but check the logistics first). There are no life guards on any of the lakes so care is needed – especially if you are swimming alone.

In the next few tips lakes with a few more activities are dicussed more fully.

5. Coniston

This lake has a boating centre for every boat you can imagine –
canoes, sail boats, motor boats, rowing boats and a few other none
boats – paddle board and bikes! It is never going to be very warm
in the water. I won't tell you this at any other lake tip entry but I
cannot emphasize this enough really.

6. Wastwater

Wastwater gets special mention because it won the best view in
Britain for the view from its shores. It is the deepest lake and it is
beside the highest English and Cumbrian mountain – Scafell Pike.
It has St Olaf's Church (one of the smallest in the country) at the
Wasdale Head end. If you need creative inspiration this is it.

7. Thirlmere

Helvellyn (the second highest peak) is Thirlmere's neighbour. It
contains the buried villages of Wythburn and Amboth so people
like to visit Wythburn church to see the exhibit there about this
story. These buried towns are, of course, where scuba divers might
like to go – but you need permission from the owners first who are
United Utilities Plc. There is a decompression chamber in Penrith
but try to avoid needing it!

8. Lake Cruises

What makes Ullswater and Windermere unique are the vintage steamers. Ullswater steamers have a varied events program on board their boats. You can also get cruises in Derwentwater (see the next tip).

Despite their primary function as a tourist attraction don't be put off using them to get around the Lakes to the various stops for the hiking that is available or taking these lake cruises with or without the meals available.

9. Derwentwater

A neighbour of Keswick this lake is incredibly popular for anything and everything. It is a tourist hotspot and it can rain anytime of year so consider visiting in an off season (i.e. not July or August) to minimize your exposure to heaving crowds and terrible traffic jams. Consequently, the area nearby has a high density of adventure companies for hiking, rafting, canoeing, biking, abseiling, climbing – the list goes on and on.

This lake has islands with rich histories to enhance the canoeing / boat tour experience. The island of St Herbert was named after the hermit monk who lived there. The ruins of the house of the Earl of Derwentwater are on Lord's Island. This lake was one of Beatrix Potter's haunts. There are excellent theatre shows available at "The

Theatre by the Lake".

However, the best feature is it's close proximity to Keswick for the old fashioned, modern, common and traditional evening lakeside picnic of fish and chips.

10. Windermere

This tip covers everything named Windermere – the lake the town and the older town Bowness-on-Windermere and the train station.

If you are in this area you are fully embedded in tourist territory but mainly because it's very pretty and there's lots to do. Attractions include The Lakes Aquarium is here at the southern tip of the Lake (tip 40) and the steamer cruises (tip 8). There are numerous swans and ducks on the lakeshores. You'll see people feeding them inappropriate food but it's better if you don't join in as it ruins there natural instincts and digestion.

Windermere town and Bowness on Windermere basically join together but there are two distinct town centres. Many buildings are from around the 1850's onwards. Windermere has the Flagship Lakeland clothing store and both have lots of boutique shops.

Taking the train to Windermere gets you right into the centre of the Lake District and it can get you to and from Manchester airport directly.

William Wordsworth

I wandered lonely as a cloud
That floats on high o'er vales and hills,
When all at once I saw a crowd,
A host of golden daffodils;
Beside the lake, beneath the trees,
Fluttering and dancing in the breeze.
Continuous as the stars that shine
and twinkle on the Milky Way,
They stretched in never-ending line
along the margin of a bay:
Ten thousand saw I at a glance,
tossing their heads in sprightly dance.
The waves beside them danced; but they
Out-did the sparkling waves in glee:
A poet could not but be gay,
in such a jocund company:
I gazed—and gazed—but little thought
what wealth the show to me had brought:
For oft, when on my couch I lie
In vacant or in pensive mood,
They flash upon that inward eye
Which is the bliss of solitude;
And then my heart with pleasure fills,
And dances with the daffodils.

Kerry Thornton

11. The Beaches

Here, as in all the lakes, the water is cold but that never seemed to be a problem when I was a child. The fun gets the better of the cold. Suitable weather for sunbathing is unlikely to be frequent but you can still get sun burnt out here.

Many of the beaches have pebbles or shingle and the sand shows when the tide goes out. Low tides tend to be quite far off shore and the sand very muddy.

St Bees, Walney Island beach and Roan Head Beach have a nature reserves the former two for bird watching and the latter for the natterjack toad.

Haverigg, Silecroft beach, Arnside beach, Silloth and Allenby beaches are the beaches not associated with a port town.

12. The Forests

Cumbria is full of forests and the distinctive treeline along the higher fells is part of what makes the scenery beautiful. You can hike or cycle through most forests. Here are some key ones to consider visiting.

Whinlatter and Grizedale are forests with a lot more short trails, child friendly activities, art and the obligatory tea rooms.

The Whinlatter information centre has the cameras on the rare Ospreys that moved into Cumbria after being re-introduced to Scotland several years ago. You can also see the osprey (by binoculars) from Bassenthwaite Lake and Dodd Wood.

If you like zip lines and canopy walks then try a forest adventure parks - Go ape in Keswick and Grizedale and Treetop nets in Windermere.

13. The Wildlife

Birds: Cumbria is a bird watchers paradise with osprey near Bassenthwaite Lake and Foulshaw Moss Nature Reserve. They can be viewed by cameras at Whinlatter Forest Visitors Centre. Other wild birds are flitting around throughout the forests but you'll have to walk fairly quietly to not scare them away. One bird you won't scare away and that you need to be careful of is the swan. They are living by Windermere Lake in large numbers (tip 10).

Mammals: For grey seals head to Walney Nature Reserve. For badgers the garden of Glen Rothay Hotel and Badger Bar and Restaurant at Rydal in Ambleside have colonies. The rest of the local animals are more secretive and it'll take some stealth on your part to see an otter, fox, rabbits, deer, hedgehogs, moles, owls, snakes and bats.

You'll definitely have more luck with farm animals – cows, sheep, pigs and horses etc at one of the open farms. These have the usual cafes, playgrounds, shops of produce and crafts (tip 35).

14. Predator Experience

Note: These experiences may not be agreeable to some animal lovers because there is human interaction with and control over the animals.

If taking chances waiting for sightings of wild animals is too time consuming then the Predator Experience in Grange-over-Sands is the place to go for Falconry experiences (including an Eagle), wolf and fox experiences. They allow you to interact pretty closely with their foxes and wolves – all for a separate fee of course.

The Cumberland Bird of Prey Centre in Carlisle and the Lakeland Bird of Prey Centre and Silverband Falconry in Penrith are alternative centres to observe falconry.

15. The Mountains

Many people come to the Lakes to climb mountains. The Lake District has the ten highest mountains in England. Scotland and Wales have higher mountains than these but the Cumbrian ones are popular for climbing, offer stunning photographs and an interesting walking and cycling trails.

Whatever walk you take the right gear is important as the weather can change quickly and don't assume that the sun won't burn you.

16. The Three Peaks Challenge

This is not for the faint hearted and unfit. It's usually done in a formal manner with guides as a fundraiser. Basically, you climb Skiddaw, Helvellyn and Scafell Pike in the same day. The third to first highest English mountains. It's hiking 32km and if you really don't think that's enough exercise you can bike or walk between the peaks.

If you are alone or a small group then you can talk to the organisers about joining other groups. This isn't a challenge that you enter without the right research and some pre-planning to reach the required fitness standards.

17. The Pennines

This mountain range is known as the backbone of England. The North Pennines were designated as an Area of Outstanding Natural Beauty (AONB) in 1988. They separate Cumbria from Yorkshire. They have the most diverse number of rare habitats in one location – moors, bogs, mountains, meadows, woods, heaths, lakes and the

High Force Waterfall.

The activities are same, same but different to the rest of the Lakes – cycling, camping, hiking, lakes, waterfalls, old towns and museums – like the Nenthead Mines site.

18. Camping or Glamping

When I was a child camping was never glamping. Camping trips I took in Cumbria across my childhood had flooded tents, blown away tents, freezing cold nightly runs to the freezing cold bathrooms, midges (small biting insects) and the uncomfortable branch or stone that couldn't be found and removed from under your bed space.

There are plenty of beautiful campsites around and obviously the intrepid readers amongst you will be fine with all these situations (and even know how to avoid them with the wonderful gear that's available nowadays) but do consider upscaling to glamping, camping barns, caravanning or staying in one of the many boutique bed and breakfasts, local hotels or hostels.

19. The Railways

Plenty of people come into the Lakes by train and get around using the trains. The West Coast Mainline can drop you off in

Oxenholme, Penrith or Carlisle but the special trains are the historic ones.

The Ravenglass to Eskdale, Lakeside and Haverthwaite are the quaint old ones that take in the scenery as the steam train takes you along the tracks.

20. The Passes

If you bring a car to the Lakes District then you might like to try driving over one of the many passes. The two that are the most challenging are Hard Knott and Wrynose followed by Kirkstone Pass, Honister Pass, Newlands Pass and Whinlatter Pass. The often single lane, steep, winding roads right in the heart of the beautiful scenery are not particularly long or dangerous if the weather is fine.

Pretty much all the roads in the Lakes District are scenic. Sometimes, even without going over a pass the driving is challenging due to narrow, winding roads with high trees (i.e. poor visibility). You will spot the locals by their high speeds! Nevertheless, the routes are not long and are filled with attractions.

Kerry Thornton

Beatrix Potter – The Tale of Peter Rabbit

Once upon a time there were four little rabbits, and their names were Flopsy, Mopsy, Cottontail, and Peter.

Kerry Thornton

21. The Arts and Artists of the Lakes

The Scenery of the Lake District is likely to inspire any creative streak within you. Many of the artists who were inspired by the Lake District did not live in the region but came for holidays and there is plenty is evidence of the landscape in their work.

Writers: Well-known writers include Beatrix Potter of the Peter Rabbit stories, John Cunliffe of Postman Pat, Arthur Ransome of "Swallows and Amazons".

Poets: William Wordsworth is a local Cumbrian and he gets his own tip (24) as a result. He is in good company with Norman Nicholson and John Ruskin.

Painters: Abbot Hall Gallery in Kendal has work by Romney, Ruskin and Harden.

Wainwright covers all the bases of guidebooks with Lakeside drawings, maps and his thoughts.

There are many modern artists with their stores throughout the region.

22. Beatrix Potter

Beatrix Potter (1866 – 1943) was originally from London. She took holidays in the Lakes District and used the scenery and wildlife to illustrate and formulate her children's stories. The most notable stories were about Peter Rabbit, Jemima Puddleduck and Squirrel Nutkin.

Her later life was spent at Hilltop farm where she saved the Herdwick sheep from extinction. This is now a National Trust property that you can visit. There is also the Beatrix Potter attraction in Bowness-on-Windermere.

There will be no shortage of shops selling her books and toys based upon those characters.

23. Brockhole

Brockhole has plenty to see and do but its lakeside walk with Beatrix Potter characters is a big draw card. This is basically a highly child friendly place (so go mid-week,, in school time if you dislike children).

There's a million activities on site so best to check the website and don't worry because the young at heart can participate in most of them.

24. Wordsworth

Wordsworth (1770 – 1850), as a local poet, had several abodes in Cumbria. Wordsworth was born in Cockermouth in a house that you can visit called (three guesses) - Wordsworth house. He lived in Dove cottage, Grasmere with his sister and died in Rydal Mount and is buried at St Oswald's Church, Grasmere. He contributed to the romantic age of poetry and was poet Laureate for Britain from 1843 until his death.

25. History

Cumbria has been inhabited for a while so you can see sights related to many different parts of its history. It really depends which period you are most interested in learning about and it's very easy to research the different ages (Bronze, Iron, Roman etc.) online. These next few tips will just cover a few gems.

26. Bronze Age History

Some of the earliest inhabitants built Castlerigg Stone Circle near Keswick and the Long Meg complex which runs alongside the River Eden, near Penrith. There are many more sites scattered around the region but these are the most striking in my opinion. These are less busy to visit than the fairly world famous stone circle "Stonehenge." Though going on a solstice is a proper party.

27. Roman History

Again there are sites upon sites of Roman ruins because this was the end of the Roman world and saw many a battle over the land. Sites that are specifically in the Lake District, if Hadrian's wall is too far away, are those at Ravenglass – ruins of a Roman bath house and a fort – and Ambleside / Kendall – Galava. Be warned these are interpretive sites for those with good imagination.

If you want to see some reasonable ruins and exhibits that are not too far beyond the Lake District, then Alauna fort and Senhouse Roman Museum in Maryport should be your next go to.

The real deal for good visual clues about how things looked is Hadrian's wall though and Birdoswald fort in Gilsland. If you want to know the truth and see the most unruined sites then the travel will be worth it.

28. Rheged

This is a historical place of power of unspecified location (it was formed in the dark ages) and an Art's Centre in Penrith. The Art's Centre is totally worth a visit if you like seeing various types of art – paintings, theatre, films etc, talks about art, workshops about art and shopping. There's loads to do here so it definitely fits beautifully as a child friendly space and rainy day option.

29. Castles

In this tip I am ignoring Roman Forts because those were covered in tip 27. This is covering the Norman and Medieval castles built from 1100's onwards. There are plenty to choose from but many are ruins.

The Norman castles that are not ruins and indeed are even operational are Carlisle castle, Appleby castle, Dalton Castle, Piel Castle, Cockermouth Castle. Advanced tour bookings are required for Appleby Castle, Dalton and Piel Castles have very limited opening times and it's very rare that there is an open day at Cockermouth Castle.

So you will have much better luck getting into a working medieval castle. Muncaster Castle is the favourite if you want to be spooked out. You can stay there overnight in the most haunted bedroom. I would love to hear from anyone that does this because I never would because my imagination is too over-active! If you want to visit in the day they have falconry shows and tours amongst other things.

30. Monasteries, Abbeys and Cathedrals

Most of these are from the Middle Ages and they have fared much better than their castle equivalents. Cartmel Priory, St Bees Priory,

Holm Cultram Abbey, Carlisle Cathedral and Lanercost Priory are the ones that remain active today so those are the first choices for visits or even attending a service to meet local people.

Of the ruined abbeys Furnace Abbey has a great visitor's centre and plenty of history and design features to talk about.

Kerry Thornton

Alfred Wainwright, The Western Fells

"The fleeting hour of life of those who love the hills is quickly spent, but the hills are eternal. Always there will be the lonely ridge, the dancing beck, the silent forest; always there will be the exhilaration of the summits. These are for the seeking, and those who seek and find while there is still time will be blessed both in mind and body."

Kerry Thornton

31. Georgian and Victorian Homes

The most obvious of these are Hilltop and Brockhole due to their Beatrix Potter connection (tip 22) and all those connected to Wordsworth – Wordsworth House, Dove Cottage and Rydal Mount (see tip 24).

The National Trust is in charge of the preservation and access to most of the stately homes from this period so the best place to start is their website. Membership gets you free admissions and covers all of Great Britain so doesn't take long to pay for itself and, of course, keeps history alive.

32. Museums

Not forgetting that the stately homes and other sites mentioned often have or are museums in themselves Cumbria has no shortage of museums. The main decision is which niche you want to explore - heritage, mining, literary, transportation or specialist museums like the Cumberland Pencil Museum in Keswick. Some are more child friendly and interactive than others.

A comprehensive Cumbrian history through artefacts is provided at the Kendal Museum. The maritime history of Cumbria is at the Maryport Maritime Museum. Keswick probably has the densest population of museums if there's nothing but rain in sight for a few days and they are all suitably different to maintain your interest.

33. Art Galleries

Art galleries that are not in a stately home or museum are also dotted around Cumbria. Carlisle, Kendal and Keswick have their own municipal art galleries. Throughout the region are galleries of local artisans.

34. Gardens and Parks

Pretty much every stately home, castle or abbey you care to visit will have gardens you can explore.

With regards to general parks there are the local playgrounds in each town with walking trails, children's play things and often sports grounds and / or tennis courts. Brockhole (tip 23) is a key one for adventure play.

35. Farms

The most child friendly farms are The Gincase Farm Park in Silloth, Walby Farm in Carlisle and Abbott Lodge in Penrith. They all go out of their way to provide a hands-on experience with the animals. Gincase has go karts and quad bikes but Walby has all bases covered with water play, pedal go-karts, animal shows, a barrel train and lots of hand's on animal experiences. If you're an adult then these places have the usual café and shop but maybe boutique butchers, cheese and oil shops in the town centres are more appealing.

36. Spas

Most of the spas are in the posher hotels and expect you to stay there as well but you can get into to some without staying on site. The benefits of staying on site is that the hotels are normally at least 4 star. There are also a few day spas around and beauty salons.

37. Family orientated activities

There have been many activities that work really well for families mentioned in other tips –The Lakes (tip 4), The Beaches (tip 11), The Forests (tip 12), The Predator Experience (tip 14), The Railways (tip 19), Brockhole (tip 23), Rheged (tip 28), The Castles (tip 29), The Museums (tip 32), The Gardens and Parks (tip 34) and The Farms (tip 35). The price range varies of course. The next tips are for the more general child friendly activities that you could find in any reasonable sized town or city.

38. Leisure Centres

There are leisure centres in most of the key towns in the region often with some combination of swimming pools, gyms and sports halls but a particularly exciting one for children is the Keswick Leisure pool because it has a wave pool and fancy slide. It is also possible to take your own food or buy food there unlike most other leisure centres.

39. General Entertainment

By this I mean ten pin - bowling alleys, roller or ice skating rinks, laser tag etc. These are all available in Cumbria but basically Carlisle has the highest density of options like these close to each other.

40. Aquariums

There are two aquariums you might like to visit – The Lakes Aquarium in Ulverston or the Lake District Coast Aquarium in Maryport. As they are at opposite ends of the region and both have put a lot of effort into their exhibits. None of them do anything too dodgy that would put off general people with concern for the welfare of animals.

Kerry Thornton

Borrowdale Sheep Counting Numbers

Yan	one
Tyan	two
Tethera	three
Methera	four
Pimp	five
Sethera	six
Lethera	seven
Hovera	eight
Dovera	nine
Dick	ten

Kerry Thornton

41. Centre Parcs

This is a very family orientated all-inclusive resort for almost millions of activities in Whinfell. There's different packages available but despite the number of activities available there you have to add most of them on so it might not work out affordable for every family holiday. It's near Penrith if you ever feel the need to leave the resort and look around.

42. Food and Drink

As a farming community most traditional Cumbrian food revolves around meat. Most of the animals that you are likely to eat will have been born and raised in the fells without much interference from antibiotics etc. The game and fish / seafood will most likely be wild caught.

Cumberland sausage is the most commonly known specialty food. It is sold in long rounds and the spices used originated via the spice trade through Whitehaven port.

There are a few locally made cheeses and butter is enhanced with brown sugar, nutmeg and rum to make rum butter for special occasions.

When I lived there food variety was extremely lacking (leaving meat and two veg as the only option) but now there are restaurants representing different cultures and addressing special dietary needs.

43. Kendal Mint Cake

Kendal Mint cake has been made in Kendal for over 100 years. It is peppermint flavoured sugar! We used to take it when we went hiking and many people still do but it won't pass any healthy food standards. You can visit the factories that produce it in…Kendal – who would have guessed?

44. The Rum Story

Whitehaven was involved in the slave trade and The Rum Story Museum does cover this alongside rum and child friendly themes around pirates. The museum might not be detailed enough about the consequences of slavery for some adults because of the intention to attract children and it may go over children's heads.

45. The Weather

"There is no such thing as bad weather, only inappropriate clothing." Sir Rannulph Fiennes.

The weather in Cumbria is notorious for being rainy – ALL THE TIME. Rain can be expected a lot over autumn, winter and spring. In summer there are some sunny days, or some sunny parts of days, and sometimes you can move from one valley to another to get away from a local rain storm. Mostly, though, the whole region is affected for days at a time. The best advice is prepare a nice mix of indoor and outdoor sights so you won't feel stuck in your accommodation. If the day is sunny use it outside – with a raincoat in your backpack! The weather reports will tell you what you need to know but always be prepared for anything when going into the fells to avoid needing to be rescued by the Mountain Rescue teams. People do die in the fells due to poor preparation and dubious decision-making.

46. Travelling with Disabilities

As I have not actually travelled with a disability myself this tip is simply because of my work as an occupational therapist brings this to mind for me.

Suitable accommodation shouldn't be too difficult to find but may be in the more premium establishments http://www.disabledholidays.com and http://www.lakedistrict-stay.co.uk list many options and can tell you about adapted transportation and equipment hire.

For general UK information might be able to help and for Cumbria specific information http://www.lakedistrict.gov.uk and http://bestlife.org.uk/ should be able to help – though the latter covers services for locals primarily.

Kerry Thornton

Regarding transportation - if you reside elsewhere in the UK you may already have passes that allow cheaper public transport so it shouldn't be too much trouble to get a NoWcard (the Cumbrian equivalent) when you arrive but I'd start with The Lake District before anything else. They have a link to their Miles without Stiles page which is all the wheelchair accessible routes in the Lakes District – and there's plenty!

Almost all of the attractions mentioned in the other tips can be accessed wheelchair user and have some support for people with other disabilities. The main issue is the transportation ones! Their websites will be the best source of information. It is going to take more research on your part unfortunately.

The main issue is that Cumbria is hilly so often the town centres are not easily accessible – Keswick is very hilly and cobbled for a large part of it. A personalized tour might be the way to go if you can afford it. Workington and Cockermouth have flat main streets if you want some shopping in commercial (the former) or boutique stores (the latter).

47. Travelling with Pets

This tip is mostly for dog owners – though I have met people travelling with cats, guinea pigs and hedgehogs before.

Dog friendly hotels that don't require your animal to be a service animal are still quite numerous you can check out http://www.petspyjamas.com which lets you book from their site and www.visitcumbria.com for accommodation and dog walks.

48. Traditions of Cumbria

I have mentioned some of our traditions - hiking the fells, eating Cumberland sausage and Kendal Mint Cake.

There are some seasonal ones like Pasche Egg Play, The Gurning Championships and the Rushbearing ceremony but the continuous ones are our Farmer's markets which have been going on since before it became trendy to have them everywhere. They happen all over the region most weekends and have anything you might possibly want – food and drinks to eat there or takeaway and arts and crafts.

A infamous tradition and one you might want to get in on is complaining (or just talking) about the weather over a nice cup of tea!

49. Language and Pronunciations

Cumbria has Celtic, Norse, Irish and Norman influences in the place names you'll see. Cumbria has so many words for the same thing – a hill, cliff or mountain can be a fell, crag, knott, howe, pike, stickle. A body of water can be a lake, mere or tarn. Often how they are written doesn't help you pronounce them or when you hear them spoken you might not connect them to the written word. Don't be afraid to ask for clarity. Getting lost on the fells is not recommended.

You may find the occasional people that you cannot understand due to the dialect and accent. For those who have a particular interest in language the

www.lakelanddialectsociety.org is a great place for more information.

For those who speak languages from other countries many leaflets and tours are available. If the non-local British cannot even say most of the place names correctly you shouldn't worry. Chat away to the locals and embrace the culture.

50. But wait…there's more…

Writing this guide has reminded me of what a fantastic place Cumbria is and shown me just how far it has come in terms of tourism / entertainment development since I was a child.

There are more attractions of course than those I have mentioned here so have a good look around for things that appeal to you and your family. With a good attitude to the risk of you spending your entire holiday in the rain you will easily be able to enjoy yourself here. As with all trips double the budget, half the luggage and turn lemons into lemonade.

Kerry Thornton

Top Reasons to Book This Trip

- Unique region of the UK in terms of geography, history, language and culture.
- British food that defies stereotypes – for meat eaters.
- So many options for any niche that interests you.
- Very family, disability and pet friendly area.
- Fresh air, beautiful scenery and wholesome entertainment give inspiration to live well.

Kerry Thornton

> TOURIST

GREATER THAN A TOURIST

Visit GreaterThanATourist.com
http://GreaterThanATourist.com

Sign up for the Greater Than a Tourist
Newsletter
http://eepurl.com/cxspyf

Follow us on Facebook:
https://www.facebook.com/GreaterThanATourist

Follow us on Pinterest:
http://pinterest.com/GreaterThanATourist

Follow us on Instagram:
http://Instagram.com/GreaterThanATourist

Kerry Thornton

> TOURIST

GREATER THAN A TOURIST

Please leave your honest review of this book on Amazon and Goodreads. Thank you.

We appreciate your positive and negative feedback as we try to provide tourist guidance in their next trip from a local.

> TOURIST

GREATER THAN A TOURIST

You can find Greater Than a Tourist books on Amazon.

Kerry Thornton

> TOURIST

GREATER THAN A TOURIST

WHERE WILL YOU TRAVEL TO NEXT?

Kerry Thornton

> TOURIST

GREATER THAN A TOURIST

Our Story

Traveling is a passion of this series creator. She studied abroad in college, and for their honeymoon Lisa and her husband toured Europe. During her travels to Malta, an older man tried to give her some advice based on his own experience living on the island since he was a young boy. She thought he was just trying to sell her something. When traveling to some places she was wary to talk to locals because she was afraid that they weren't being genuine. She created this book series to give you as a tourist an inside view on the place you are exploring and the ability to learn what locals would like to tell tourist. A topic that they are very passionate about.

Kerry Thornton

> TOURIST

GREATER THAN A TOURIST

Notes

Made in United States
Orlando, FL
08 March 2022

15510737R00048